Poetry Collections by Lesléa Newman

I Carry My Mother

October Mourning: A Song for Matthew Shepard
(novel-in-verse)

I Remember: Hachiko Speaks
(chapbook)

Nobody's Mother

Signs of Love

Still Life With Buddy

The Little Butch Book

Lovely

Lovely

poems by

Lesléa Newman

HEADMISTRESS PRESS

Copyright © 2018 by Lesléa Newman
All rights reserved.

ISBN-13: 978-0998761046
ISBN-10: 0998761044

This book may not be reproduced, in whole or in part, including illustrations, in any form (beyond that permitted by Sections 107 and 108 of the U.S. Copyright Law and except by reviewers for the public press), without written permission from the publishers.

"My Mother's Stories" from *Soap Opera Confidential: Writers and Soap Insiders on Why We'll Tune in Tomorrow as the World Turns Restlessly by the Guiding Light of Our Lives* © 2017 Edited by Elizabeth Searle and Suzanne Stempek Shea. By permission of McFarland & Company, Inc, Box 611, Jefferson NC 28640. www.mcfarlandpub.com

Cover art © 2012 Carol Marine, "Pink Power." Oil on gessoboard 6x6 in. carolmarine.com

Cover & book design by Mary Meriam.

PUBLISHER
Headmistress Press
60 Shipview Lane
Sequim, WA 98382
Telephone: 917-428-8312
Email: headmistresspress@gmail.com
Website: headmistresspress.blogspot.com

for Mary Grace Newman Vazquez

Table Of Contents

PART I: FLYING TOWARD HOME
Thirteen Ways Of Looking At A Blackboard	1
Home Safe	4
First Death	9
Maidel	12
My Mother Cups Her Hand	15
My Mother's Stories	16
The Price	17
Mourning Song	18
The Chanukah Game	19

PART II: FAIREST OF THEM ALL
1955- 2001: A Hair Odyssey	23
And Now Let Us Sing	26
May Day	29
Between Flights	30
Mirror, Mirror	32
Old Age	33
After The Blizzard, Outside My Window	34
Statue	35
Blessed Are The Weeds	36

PART III: LEAVING BODIES BEHIND
Dear Vincent	39
Near Death Experience	42
That Night	44
Teen Angels	45
Wedding/Funeral March	48
Poem For Two Dogs Hanged In Salem, Massachusetts, 1692	49
Viet Nam	51
A Farewell To Arms	53

PART IV: ONCE UPON A TIME

Sleepaway Camp, 1969	57
Somebody	59
Somebody's Son	61
Your Loss: To The Lovely Butch In Front Of Me At The A&P	63
Thirteen Ways of Looking At A Poet	64
Insomnia	67
Ode To Chocolate	69
Ode To A Knish Shop	71
Ode to Mangoes	72
Pear	73
According To Bread	74

PART V: NASTY WOMEN

To Have And To Hold	77
Seduction In Red	78
Paradise Found	79
Night On The Town	80
I Want To Stay Up Talking But	81
The Coming Storm	82
Love Shampoo	83
Ghazal For My Beloved	84
What I Love	85
The Writer And The Messenger	86
Why I Always Wear Makeup	89

Notes	90
Acknowledgements	91
About The Author	93

"She is very lovely and mine which is very lovely."
—Gertrude Stein

PART I: FLYING TOWARD HOME

Thirteen Ways Of Looking At A Blackboard

I
Among twenty crowded classrooms
The only sound
Was the rat-tat-tat
Of the white stick of chalk
Against the black blackboard.

II
I was of three minds,
Like the multiple-choice question
With three incorrect answers
Scrawled upon the blackboard.

III
The eraser whirled across the blackboard.
It was a small part of the pantomime.

IV
A teacher and her classroom
Are one.
A teacher and her classroom and her blackboard
Are one.

V
I do not know which I dread more,
The start of the lesson
Or the end of the lesson.
The blackboard covered with problems
Or just erased.

VI
Foreign words filled the blackboard
In a curled and swirling script.
The shadow of the teacher
Paced to and fro
Her mood was indecipherable.

VII
Oh restless children at your wooden desks
Why do you stare out the window at the sky?
Do you not see the blank blackboard before you
Waiting like a Buddha for your attention?

VIII
I know great lines from great poetry
And my times-tables up through twelve.
But I know, too,
That the blackboard is involved
In everything I know.

IX
When the blackboard disappeared
From the front of the classroom,
It marked the end of one of many eras.

X
At the sight of the cracked blackboard
Lying on the curb with the trash,
Even the most overworked, underpaid teacher
Would cry out sharply.

XI
She dreamt she was back
In her third grade classroom
And a great fear pierced her
As she watched herself vanish
Into the bottomless black hole
Of the blackboard.

XII
The classroom is empty.
The blackboard must be lonely.

XIII
It was the end of the school year
All year long.
We were graduating
And we were going to graduate.
The blackboard sat
Covered in chalk dust.

Home Safe

Little Girl Blue,
What happened to you?
Who was it? Who?
And what did he do?

I was seven. Or eight.
Young enough to be still
unashamed of my body.

He was five. Or six.
Old enough to know a boy
could do whatever he wanted

to a girl who wasn't
the prettiest, the skinniest
the fairest in the land.

It was the children's hour,
that wild blue interlude
between supper and bedtime

when the moms were in their kitchens
washing off the dishes, and the dads
were in their dens gazing at TV.

All us kids were in the park
except for Mindy Finkelstein
whose father made her lie down

for an entire hour after she ate
so she could "digest." The rest
of us huddled close together

like a rack of pool balls
until Tommy Batista gave the signal
and we broke, scattering

across the green felt grass screeching
with joy, both the chasers and the chased.
We played Running Bases, TV Tag,

Ring-a-levio, Fox-and-Geese.
The sun went down. The breeze picked up.
Frogs croaked. Peepers peeped.

I was flying towards home
base which was Mrs. Barricolli's back yard.
We called her Mrs. Macaroni

which she knew and didn't mind.
All I had to do was tag the big oak tree
behind her two-car garage and I'd be safe.

I ran as if my life depended on it
and crashed into a boy
and tumbled to the ground.

He climbed on top of me.
He wasn't very heavy.
His head blocked out the last drop of sun.

Little Girl Blue,
Who was it? Who?

He didn't live on our block.
He was nobody's kid brother.
He didn't play by the rules.

He had grass stains on his dungarees,
blond Dennis the Menace hair
that whipped in the wind,

a small cut on his chin.
Big blue eyes. He was smaller
than me. But stronger.

Little Girl Blue,
What did he do?

He knew no one
else was around.
He knew I was cornered.

He knew he held me
in the grubby palm
of his dirt-streaked hand

which snaked its way
between my legs
where his curious fingers

furled and unfurled
curled and uncurled
like the sea anemone

I had once seen on a class trip
to the Bronx zoo.
That day I'd stood perfectly still

my hands and face pressed
against the cool glass,
hypnotized, mesmerized,

just as I was right now
as his fingers found that strange spot
inside me, a foreign country

I never knew existed,
a place that felt so good
I knew right away it was bad.

His fingers so gentle
against the thin seam of my pedal pushers
fluttering rippling tickling.

Little Girl Blue
What did you do?

I didn't move
for a minute, an hour,
a lifetime, until something

streaked by—a firefly? a dog?
another kid? my big brother?
The boy took off and I crawled

to the tree. Home safe.
I waited until the lights
came on in the houses

all around me, and the moms
called their kids home
and the dads put out the trash.

Little Girl Blue
then what did you do?

I dragged my body home
like a bulky bag of groceries
I had trouble holding in my arms.

I never played in the park
again. I had homework, a headache,
a bellyache, I had to lie

down and digest
what had happened
in Mrs. Macaroni's back yard.

It took me fifty years
to realize how hurt
that little boy must have been.

Little Boy Blue,
What happened to you?
Who was it? Who?
And what did they do?

First Death

> "After the first death, there is no other."
> —Dylan Thomas

On the day Mimi Schechter returned to us
we became the pack of wild animals
our parents always said we'd grow up to be.

Truthfully, we hadn't noticed she'd been gone
for six months. Plain as the brown lunch sack
she clutched in one hand, she stood out

of our way as we did what kids do while waiting
to be scooped up by a yellow school bus:
the boys chased the girls worthy of being chased,

the girls ran shrieking in terrified joy, and the rest
of us pretended not to care that no one cared
enough about us to steal our books or pull our hair.

Mimi Schechter swayed like a small tree trembling
in the wind, her eyes wide in her pale, chalky face
looking much older than her scant seven years.

She wasn't as I remembered her, though I did not
remember her at all. Somehow she had turned
into her own grandmother, her features faded

and her eyebrows completely gone like a lesson
on the blackboard recently erased. And her hair—
it wasn't little kid's hair anymore. It was

too perfect, smooth and sleek and straight,
each strand turning under her chin just so
like those high-kicking Rockettes, all in a row.

It's a wig, I thought, and as though Danny Lieberman could read
my mind, he gave up chasing Amy Sabatelli, spun
on his heels, and snatched Mimi Schechter's wig with a whoop

and a holler, throwing his prize straight up in the air.
Mimi Schechter's hair hovered in the blue suburban sky
blocking out the sun for a split second before it fell like a shot

bird. Another boy caught it and gave it back
to Danny who tossed it to another kid who tossed it
to another kid, while Mimi Schechter just stood there

in all her bald-headed glory and despair. The sight
was so frightening it made someone shout
"Bowling head! Bowling head!" and not one of us

had the courage to not join in. We laughed and tossed
that wig back and forth, back and forth until someone caught
sight of our school bus rounding the corner and we all fell

into an orderly line except for Mimi Schechter who ran
home weeping. "Cry Baby! Cry Baby!" we called
as each one of us walked past Mimi Schechter's wig

sprawled on the ground like an injured animal
run over by one of our mother's cars.
And that was that. Mimi Schechter never came back

to school and no one knew what happened
to her until two months later when the principal
made a crackly request over the PA system

after we'd said the Pledge of Allegiance,
asking for a moment of silence for our good friend
Mimi Schechter who had just that morning

died. Died! I didn't know anyone who was dead and I ran home
bursting with the news. "Mom, you'll never guess!" I yelled,
as if I'd received an "A" on my spelling test.

My mother was in the kitchen, tethered to the phone
when I announced, "Mimi Schechter died!" and then collapsed
in a fit of giggles. She hung up quickly and stared

at her beast of a daughter, now doubled over and howling
with laughter like an unhinged hyena. I deserved
the slap she gave me on behalf of Mimi Schechter

Mimi Schechter who deserved a little respect from me
Mimi Schechter whose tear-streaked face I still see
Mimi Schechter, my first death, November 18, 1963.

Maidel

Don't fill up on the bread. Don't chew with your mouth open. Get your elbows off the table. Get your hair out of your eyes. You have such a pretty face, if only you'd lose some weight. Finish what's on your plate; children in Europe are starving. There's no such thing as a free lunch.

If you don't like the table you're shown to, tell the maître d', "Take me to the table you were saving in case I didn't like this one." If you don't have anything nice to say, sit next to me. You can't with one tuchus dance at two weddings. That's the way the matzo crumbles. Brooklyn wasn't built in a day. Don't stand on ceremony. Don't cut off your nose to spite your face. There's no problem so terrible it can't get worse.

Drink hot coffee in the summer, it will cool you down. Get pregnant in the fall, give birth in the spring. Heartburn means you'll have a hairy baby. I ate nothing but Tums when I was pregnant with you. Boys are easier to raise than girls. Just wait till you have a daughter. *But Mom, I don't want to have children.* Don't talk to me in that tone of voice. You only think you know what's best for you. Don't get smart with me. You're too smart for your own good.

Don't stick anything in your ear except your washcloth or your elbow. Keep your legs together. Don't talk to strangers.

Never kid a kidder. Someday you'll thank me for this. I need this like I need a hole in the head. This hurts me more than it hurts you. Just wait till your father gets home. Stop crying or I'll give you something to really cry about. You're too sensitive. I only want you should be happy.

Nothing is worth mortgaging your teeth over. Never buy retail. Cheap is expensive. You get what you pay for. If the shoe fits, buy it in black, brown, and navy. Everything comes back in style if you wait long enough. If it can't hurt you and you don't have to feed it, leave it alone. There's no such thing as an expiration date. Behave yourself or we'll bring you back to Macy's. Money doesn't grow on trees. Your father and I aren't made of money. It's just as easy to marry rich as it is to marry poor.

Wash the fruit. If you can't go, eat an apple. If you're going too much, eat a banana. Breakfast is the most important meal of the day. If you're hungry, eat a piece of celery. A woman can never be too thin or too rich. Rich or poor, it's good to have money. Stand up straight, it will make you look slimmer. A little lipstick never hurt anybody. Would it kill you to smile once in a while? Gay used to mean happy. Nobody likes a sour puss.

I'm cold, go put on a sweater. Don't sit so close to the television. Don't stand so close to the microwave. The early bird catches the worm. *But Mom, I don't like worms.* You're not going out of the house looking like that. As long as you live under my roof, you'll do as I tell you. Do as I say, not as I do. Learn to type, you need something to fall back on. Any idiot can write a book.

If you were really a peacenik you wouldn't wear army pants. Why do you make yourself as ugly as possible? Don't be such a pill. You get more flies with honey. *But Mom, who wants flies?* Spit out that gum, you look like a cow.

I'm telling you this for your own good. You don't know how good you have it. Carry some mad money in the bottom of your shoe. Carry an umbrella. Save something for a rainy day. Cover your mouth when you sneeze. Put on a bra. Always wear clean underwear. You never know when you're going to wind up in a ditch. If it ain't broke, don't fix it. If it is broke, give it to me; I'll fix it. Being a mother means never having to say you're sorry. Am I right or am I right? Everyone is entitled to my opinion. It is what it is. Enough is enough.

My Mother Cups Her Hand

My mother cups her hand around my cheek
And draws me close until we're head to head
Neither one of us can bear to speak

 We know that she'll be dead within a week
And both of us believe that dead is dead
My mother cups her hand around my cheek

I swallow back a monumental shriek
And curse the goddamn tumors that have spread
Neither one of us can bear to speak

She stares at me, her brown eyes growing bleak
What's left to say forever left unsaid
My mother cups her hand around my cheek

We know that death will creep in like a sneak
And snatch my mother right up from her bed
Neither one of us can bear to speak

In the face of death we've both grown meek
The heavy silence blankets us with dread
My mother cups her hand around my cheek
Neither one of us can bear to speak

My Mother's Stories

are her *Passions*, she reminds me
watching TV in her *General Hospital* bed
and tuning out *The Doctors* and *The Nurses*
with their masked *Hidden Faces*
who enter her room to *Soap* up and
cast *Dark Shadows* across *The Days Of Our Lives*.

My mother is a *Valiant Lady* with *One Life To Live*,
On The Edge Of Night. *As The World Turns*,
and her *Moment of Truth* looms large, she shrinks
to her *Bare Essence*, frail as a *Flame In The Wind*
clinging to her *Search for Tomorrow*
and a *Bright Promise* for *Another World*.

"*The First Hundred Years* are the hardest," she jokes
with her oncologist, a *Young Doctor Malone*. "I had
The Best Of Everything. *Love Is A Many Splendored Thing*.
Here are *All My Children: The Young and The Restless*.
The Bold and The Beautiful. *This Is Where The Heart Is*.
I never wanted *Another Life*."

Her show over, my mother stares out the *Golden Windows*
searching for her *Guiding Light* on *The Clear Horizon*.
We remain *A World Apart* watching her *Rough Crossing*
over *Paradise Bay* across the *Highway To The Stars*.
The Secret Storm carries her *Three Steps To Heaven*
and she becomes for *Generations, A Woman to Remember*.

The Price

"I'm not going to mortgage
my teeth for that," said my mother
and the lovely red wool coat

with four shiny black buttons
that perfectly matched my Mary Janes
and the real fur collar soft

as my puppy dog's silky brown ear
was returned to the rack and that
was that. Tears were to no avail.

"Money doesn't grow on trees. Stop
crying or I'll give you something
to really cry about." Her voice

sharp as a door slamming shut.
Half a century later, I have my own
mortgage, a back yard of trees

with leaves the color of money
and something to really cry about,
no mother to call on the phone

to share the good news: I found
the red winter coat of my dreams
today, on sale, two for the price of one.

Mourning Song

Who was it who slithered in stealth as a thief
And snatched up my mother from deep underneath
My sniveling father and I stuffed with grief
That was soon nudged aside by our brash disbelief?

Who hung grief round my neck like a needling wreath,
Cutting my flesh with its milky white teeth,
Unearthing a wealth of unwelcome relief
Lying in wait down beneath the beneath?

Is it true guilt's no good for my shriveling health?
Can I stash it away like a book on a shelf?
Could I have done more before my mother's death?
Will I wrestle that question till my dying breath?

And if I dash out and by chance catch that thief
And give him the gift of my guilt and my grief,
Will I be set free from my rash disbelief
To dive into the darkness that lurks underneath?

The Chanukah Game

Our mother fries golden latkes,
Our father spins wooden dreidels,

Our grandmother gives out bittersweet gelt,
And my brother and I sit still for once

To play the Chanukah game.
Perched on sticky vinyl chairs

At the rickety kitchen table,
Elbows on placemats, chins resting on fists,

My brother picks the tall white *shamash,*
I choose the blue candle on the end.

We fix our eyes on the dull brass menorah:
Whose flame will last the longest?

Fifty years flicker by.
My Persian cat turns twenty,

My brother's son becomes a man,
Our mother and grandmother play Mah Jongg in heaven,

Our father grows old as time and older still,
And Chanukah comes round again.

My brother and I live in different states.
We light the menorah in separate houses,

We sing the blessing over the phone,
We hold the line as the candles burn down.

Whose flame will last the longest?
God only knows.

PART II: FAIREST OF THEM ALL

1955-2001: A Hair Odyssey

I
"The day I gave birth to you,
you had such beautiful, dark curly hair
the nurses all took turns combing it.
You left the hospital with a ponytail
tied up in a pink ribbon and I was so happy
you were a girl
I cried."

II
I cry
every morning before high school
because of my hair
my hair:
frizz bomb
kinky head
Jew fro
the human barometer
Every night I set it on rollers the size of orange juice cans
wrap it around my head with larger-than-life bobby pins
scotch-tape it to my forehead and cheeks
flatten it out along my mother's ironing board
only to have it *boing!* back to its curly frizzy, kinky Jewish self
every goddamn morning.

III
On a kibbutz in Israel I live in a room
with six other American girls
all of us fascinated by Mona.
Mona has straight hair!

How does she do it?
We watch, mesmerized
as she divides her waist-length tresses
into dozens of sections one-inch thick
and runs the blow dryer up and down each one
every morning starting at 4:00 a.m.
in order to be ready for breakfast at 6:00.
Two hours—is it worth it?
You bet.
The next morning, we are all up at 4:00
fighting over the one outlet in the room
having flown halfway around the world
just to learn how to straighten our hair.

IV
The first thing I do
when I realize I am a lesbian
is hack off my hair.
The second thing I do
is cry.

V
"Is that a perm?"
Yes.
"How long have you had it?"
Forty-five years.

VI
Out of nowhere, a gray hair.
Then another. And another.
I can't believe it.
The words I spat at my mother

as an arrogant teen
come racing back to me:
"Women shouldn't dye their hair.
It's so unnatural."
How did she put up with me?
Sitting at the hairdresser's
under a stark white light
before an unforgiving mirror,
a lavender smock draped about my neck
my hair plastered back from my face
with cold, wet goo,
I look like my mother:
vulnerable, exposed, ashamed.

VII
Finally, we are friends
my hair and I
my dyed dark brown chin-length hair
framing my face in soft curls
sometimes held back
with a hair band or clip
sometimes frizzy in the heat
sometimes flat in the cold
always growing
always changing
unruly
unmanageable
unpredictable
like me.

And Now Let Us Sing

the praises of the one white whisker
that appeared out of nowhere
on the 83rd day of my 61st year.

I swear it wasn't there the day before
when I studied the lines of my face
in the bathroom mirror as I do

every morning, the same way
I peer into my closet
and refrigerator hoping

something gorgeous or delicious
will magically appear: presto
change-o, hocus pocus

abracadabra, ladies and gentleman
please hold your applause
we need absolute silence,

though I wouldn't blame you
for gasping at the sight
of the one thick bristle

the length of a baby's eyelash
sticking straight out
of the dark brown dot

on the southwest corner of my chinny
chin chin which I'd always thought of
as a beauty mark and of which I'd been

quite fond, it was a mark of distinction,
it made me feel Marilyn Monroe-ish,
it had been with me since the beginning

and never surprised me or betrayed me
like it did the morning
it birthed this unexpected, uninvited

but nevertheless welcome gift
because it brought with it
a memory of my mother

lying in her hospital bed
as still as a flattened pillow
before bolting up from a deep sleep,

beckoning me to her side,
and pointing to a similar hair
sticking out of her cheek.

Without a word I knew
what she wanted me to do:
fetch a pair of tweezers

and a mirror so weak as she was
she could yank that sucker out
with a surgeon's precision

then hand over her implements
and sleep for the rest of the day
with a sweet little smile

on her eggshell smooth face,
only to open her eyes at dusk
and make me promise

that when she was no longer
able to do for herself
that I would do what she had just done.

Cross my heart and hope to die
I thought but did not say
as she lay there day after day

and I kept a watchful eye
on the X-marks-the-spot
spot on the map of her left cheek,

searching for that sharp wiry quill
which never appeared again
until today when it poked

itself out of my very own face:
Surprise! Here I am!
hi Mom

May Day

All winter long the old apple tree waits
outside my window poised like a prima ballerina
its twisted trunk a delicate arch
its bare branches holding an elegant pose.
Still, still, still, until today
when God tapped Her baton
and the tree leapt to life
covered with scores of pink blossoms
that rustled sweetly in the breeze
like a thousand dancers in taffeta skirts
clustered before a dressing room
mirror mirror on the wall
each one the fairest of them all.
Oh, I too was once a girl
with ribbons streaming through my hair
with a spring in my step
and satin slippers on my feet
completely wrapped up in my own dark beauty
until it all unraveled and I was left out in the cold.
So come, come, come rush outside with me.
Bow your head and breathe, breathe deep.
Reach out your arms and take what is given.
It isn't too late to accept the bouquet.

Between Flights

> "I knew a woman, lovely in her bones"
> —Theodore Roethke

And so I name them Lovely and Lovelier
these two young beauties sitting before me
at the airport, the older one braiding

the younger one's hair. Lovely is perched
on the edge of womanhood as surely
as she is perched on the edge

of her black vinyl seat, lost
in concentration as she combs
her fingers through Lovelier's hair

separating it into several hanks
and holding them aloft like the reins
of a filly who has consented to be tamed.

Lovelier kneels on the floor
back straight and neck elongated
like a Modigliani model

a Mona Lisa smile playing
across her glossy lips.
Or perhaps I am wrong.

Perhaps the older one is Lovelier
her elegant arms drifting up and down
like a principal dancer

as she weaves Lovely's hair
into an intricate French braid
too stylish for her young

face which still boasts freckles
across her nose like the spots
of a doe too small to leave her mother.

And now the braid is done
and the younger girl lifts
one hand to the side of her head

patting it gently to make sure
it is perfect as she is perfect,
and the older girl sits back

to admire the good work she has done,
and I, who was once just as lovely
if not lovelier than the two of them

put together, sally forth
toward my own gate as they rise
and fly past me to soar into their lives.

Mirror, Mirror

Mirror, mirror, on the wall
I look to you to speak the truth:
Who's the fairest of them all?

My dance card full at every ball
I sparkled like a jewel with youth,
Mirror, mirror on the wall.

I once inspired men to brawl,
my brand new beauty sleek and smooth
I was the fairest of them all.

But now old age has come to call
and I've grown longer in the tooth,
Mirror, mirror on the wall.

I spent a fortune at the mall
and hours in a make up booth,
Am I the fairest of them all?

Shrouded in a wrinkled pall
I beg you not to be uncouth:
Mirror, mirror on the wall,
Say I'm the fairest of them all.

Old Age

The cat, so afraid of an ice cube's sharp clink,
now stirs not a hair as I mix a stiff drink.

After the Blizzard, Outside My Window

The still white street a-glitter in the sun
is traversed by a small tuxedo cat
who tiptoes gently as a solemn nun
then leaps and rolls, a circus acrobat.
His black fur dusted with a coat of snow
he sits to give his left hind leg a lick
till startled by the cawing of a crow
he looks about him: could this be a trick?
And now the squirrel waves her wind blown tail
And now the sparrow sings her morning song
And now my neighbor comes out for his mail
And now the black cat stands and moves along
To think that all of this is mine for free,
The world is so much better than TV.

Statue

All winter long Mary guards
the garden, standing up
to her stone cold shoulders
in glistening white snow
pure as they say she was
so many centuries ago.
She knows better
than to set them straight.
She knows they need her
to believe in miracles
like the return of spring
which always comes
on the day their hope
vanishes like melted snow,
and in its place a crocus
yellow as butter blooming
at her concrete feet.

Blessed Are The Weeds

For they show up wherever they damn well please
For they are not afraid to take up space

For they are tickled by spring breezes and summer rain
For they always lift their golden heads toward the sun

For they wake up early and stay up late
For they do not consider any hour ungodly

For they dig down deep
For they respect their roots

For they believe in their wild and glorious beauty
For they make friends with the lowly, lonely worm

For they can weather any and every storm
For they stand up tall and unafraid

For they are good-natured, with few and simple needs
For they are happy wherever they find themselves

For they know the dignity of days spent in silence
For they don't care what others say or think

For they know when to hold fast and when to let go
For they yield when necessary without complaint

For they accept their days are precious and numbered
For they grow fruitful and multiply as they are commanded

For they bring me to my humble, bony knees
For they lie down gently in my naked, aching arms

PART III: LEAVING BODIES BEHIND

Dear Vincent

I am standing before a cypress tree
planted firmly on the wall
of the Clark Art Institute.

Between me and the tree, a sea
of blonde heads swing back and forth
like a sun-stroked field of wheat

you might have painted long ago.
I join the herd of New York ladies
moving en masse from painting

to painting, trailing behind
like a tall dark shadow, listening
to their chatter. "Vincent painted

this one when he first moved to Paris."
"Vincent never really liked this one."
Ah, Vinnie, we hardly knew ye

and what would you make of all
this fuss? Your humble canvasses
flew across the sea in a silver plane

(Vincent, can you imagine?)
and were carefully hung on the wall
of the Clark Art Institute

for the sole purpose of gazing
at us while we gaze at them
feeling so pleased with ourselves

for spending the day
staring at lovely works of art
instead of our computer screens

scrolling through Facebook
where many of us will show up
snapped in front of a floor-to-ceiling

replica of *Green Wheat Fields, Auvers*
hoping to impress our two-thousand friends.
But that comes later, for now

museum fatigue has set in
so after a trip to the gift shop
where we buy Sunflower dish towels

and Starry Night magnets
we file into the café to purchase
a brown bag lunch of wheatberry

salad, a plump, still life-worthy plum
and a chocolate chip cookie so large
it fills us with delight and dismay.

"Oh I can't eat this. So many calories."
"Oh come on. You're on vacation."
"Oh, all right. Just this once."

We lumber outside to collapse
onto Adirondack chairs scattered
across the lawn of the Clark Art Institute

under the impossibly blue summer sky
dotted with clouds like clotted cream
a scene you would have painted

for surely, Vincent, you would find us
pleasing to your palette. *Les Femmes
en Plein Air* you might call us

or simply *Le Dejeuner*. And as we
nibble on cookies, dab our mouths
with scratchy brown paper napkins,

re-apply poppy red lipstick and lift
our faces towards the blazing sun
that burns swirling circles

of orange and yellow into
our shuttered fluttering eyelids
we can't help but wonder:

was it the right ear, or the left,
dear Vincent, and would you
have cut it off for me?

Near Death Experience

End of August. New York City. I wake up. In a sweat. Hot as hell. Turn back over. Lift my head. See the clock. Ten past nine. Late for work. Throw on clothes. Grab my purse. Slam the door. Take the stairs. Hit the street. Hit a wall. Why the crowd? God it's hot. Can't push through. "What's the deal?" "Check it out." Points to sky. I look up. See a man. On the roof. "Says he'll jump." "Oh my God." Here come cops. One goes in. One stays back. Barks out, "Move." No one moves. Just the man. On the roof. He looks down. Then he waves. Some wave back. He looks pleased. Steps toward us. We step back. With a gasp. Cop yells "Stop!" Man stands still. Then he laughs. Starts to dance. Near the edge. Struts his stuff. Back and forth. Flaps his arms. Like a bird. "What's he on?" "Don't ask me." "Will he jump?" "Hard to tell." "What's his name?" "No one knows." My neck hurts. Sweat pours down. Dress is soaked. Late for work. Could get canned. What do to? There's a man. On the roof. He steps back. Out of sight. Is he gone? No, he's back. On the roof. Near the edge. Whips off shirt. Twirls it twice. Swings his hips. Shakes his butt. Crowd goes wild. "Hey, Big Spender." "Take it off." "Go, go, go." Man drops shirt. Man drops pants. Clasps his hands. Holds them high. Like a champ. Turns full circle. In slow motion. Big beer belly. Big white ass. Big dumb grin. Where's that cop? There's a man. With no clothes. On the roof. Near the edge. Now a woman. Two flights down. In the window. Gives a shriek. "Earl, you fool." "Shut up, bitch." "You shut up." "Go to hell." "Kiss my ass." Slams down window. Earl's face drops. Hangs his head. What to do? Now a chant. From the crowd. "We want Earl! We want Earl!" Earl looks up. Great big smile. Lifts his foot. Puts it down. On the edge. Of the roof. Starts to sway. Spreads his arms. Will he fall? Will he fly? What to do? There's a man. On the roof. With no clothes. Near the edge. There's a crowd. On the street. "We want Earl! We want Earl!" I feel faint. Turn to leave. Bump a man. In a suit. "Hey, watch out." Scowls at me. Then he smiles. At his pal. In a suit. Both hands full. "Here's your coffee." "Thanks a lot." "Want a donut?" "Sure, why not?" "What'd I miss?" "Not a thing." "Still up there?" "Big as life." "Wish he'd hurry." "Move it, Earl." "Let's go, buddy." "Come on, jump!" Are they nuts? Earl looks out. At the crowd. Steps right up. To the edge. Curls his toes. Bends his knees. Arms out straight. Chin to chest. Will he jump? Will he dive? Where's his wife? Where's the cop? What to do? There's a man. On the roof. With no clothes. On the edge. I can't look. Close my eyes. Pray like hell. Hope to God.

That Night

> "Fifty people are dead after a man opened fire early Sunday inside a gay nightclub in Orlando"
> —*New York Times,* June 12, 2016

That night we drank a few shots at the bar
That night we were shot many times at the bar

That night the bartender cried, "Last call!"
That night we frantically made last calls

That night the music pulsed through our veins
That night the bullets tore through our veins

That night we got down and sweated together
That night we fell down and bled together

That night the bartender mixed Bloody Marys
That night the killer fixed bloody Marys

That night some of us shared our first kiss
That night all of us shared our last kiss

That night we danced in each other's arms
That night we died in each other's arms

That night turned into a cloud-streaked morning
That night turned into a tear-streaked mourning

Teen Angels

Raymond Chase
Tyler Clementi
Billy Lucas
Asher Brown
Seth Walsh
Carl Walker-Hoover

19 years old
18 years old
15 years old
13 years old
13 years old
11 years old

Raymond Chase
Tyler Clementi
Billy Lucas
Asher Brown
Seth Walsh
Carl Walker-Hoover

"Fag"
"Faggot"
"Fairy"
"Sissy"
"Homo"
"Queer"

Raymond Chase
Tyler Clementi
Billy Lucas
Asher Brown
Seth Walsh
Carl Walker-Hoover

punched
slapped
kicked
chased
tackled
stripped

Raymond Chase
Tyler Clementi
Billy Lucas
Asher Brown
Seth Walsh
Carl Walker-Hoover

ashamed
afraid
enraged
depressed
defeated
alone

Raymond Chase
Tyler Clementi
Billy Lucas
Asher Brown
Seth Walsh
Carl Walker-Hoover

Hanged himself
Drowned himself
Hanged himself
Shot himself
Hanged himself
Hanged himself

Raymond Chase
Tyler Clementi
Billy Lucas
Asher Brown
Seth Walsh
Carl Walker-Hoover

Friend
Brother
Cousin
Teammate
Classmate
Mama's Boy

Wedding/Funeral March

> "In March 2012, Amina Filali, a 16-year-old Moroccan girl, committed suicide after she was forced to marry her rapist."
> —*The World Post,* February 17, 2017

Here comes the Bride, so terrified,
Broken and battered and made to abide.
Throat full of bile, she trips down the aisle,
Her shame and her sorrow inflamed by his smile.

There goes the Bride, for three years she's cried,
Each night she is forced to lie down by his side.
She can't be his wife. She picks up a knife,
Knowing that Death can be no worse than Life.

Poem For Two Dogs Hanged in Salem, Massachusetts, 1692

Did they hang
their heads
as good dogs do
when they're eager
to make it easy
for someone to slip
a collar
or a rope
around their furry necks

Did they prance
along proudly
as happy dogs do
when they trot
beside a friend
or stranger
who's taking them
away
for a nice long walk

Did they give
sloppy kisses
as loving dogs do
when a kind man
or a gruff man
kneels down
beside them
and says *sit*
and *stay*

Did they shake
all over
as frightened dogs do
when they're startled
by thunder or lightning
or black hoods
placed over their heads
making everything too quiet
and dark

Did they swing
their tails
as innocent dogs do
when they're puzzled
or confused
but still
trusting those near
will bring them
no harm

Or did they bare
their teeth
growl and leap
to snap at the Hangman
before he strung them up
and they rose
to Heaven
leaving bodies behind
to be buried like bones

Viet Nam

The first time Bud came home
with me
I tried not to look
surprised
when he
unbuttoned his shirt
unzipped his pants
unfastened his left leg
and hopped
into bed
beside me

"Wanna hump the stump?"
he asked. I did
what any red-blooded
American girl would do.
Twice.
Then we slept until Bud woke
screaming and I held him
close as the baby
he'd fathered
and left behind
half a world away

In the morning Bud left
his dog tags
around my neck
while he washed up
and I sat down

and lifted his leg
by the foot
of my bed
I laid it across my lap
It was cold and smooth
and hard and comforting

That was thirty-eight years ago
I can't recall Bud's last name
or the color of his eyes
But the weight of that leg
in my lap
is lodged in my brain
like a bullet
shot from the M-16
he carried all those months
before the first and only time
Bud came home with me

A Farewell To Arms

for Andrea Ayvazian

No more bullets, no more bombs,
No more broken-hearted moms

No more shrapnel, no more guns,
No more sacrificing sons

No more pistols, no more knives,
No more taking fathers' lives

No more stoning, no more spears,
No more daughters shedding tears

No more missiles, no more hits,
No more brothers blown to bits

No more snipers, no more spies,
No more sisters' anguished cries

No more wounded, no more burned,
No more letters marked "returned"

No more napalm, no more screams,
No more sweethearts' shattered dreams

No more torture, no more fists,
No more names on "missing" lists

No more warships, no more planes,
No more shipping home remains

No more hatred, no more blame,
No more killing in God's name

No more bodies, no more coffins,
No more widows, no more orphans

No more bad news at the door,
No more bloodshed, no more war.

PART IV: ONCE UPON A TIME

Sleepaway Camp, 1969

He was black
I was white
He was a cook
I was a camper
We kissed by the lake
one hot August night

I remember that night
being very black
down by the lake
only one white
star shining above the camp
above me above the cook

We dared to cook
something up that night
the brazen camper
the handsome black
cook still in his white
apron down by the lake

The camp was called Silver Lake
I don't recall the cook's
name only his white
apron slicing the night
like a beacon in the blackness
as we snuck through camp

away from the other campers
to the tiny rippling lake
The water looked black
black as the cook
black as the night
only my skin was white

Of course I was white
like all the other campers
asleep in their bunks the night
I lay down at the lake
and reached up for the cook
and all his glorious blackness

black sky   white moon
tender cook   happy camper
sultry lake   racy night

Somebody

September 11, 2001

How on earth
can a sky be
as clear and blue
as the eyes
of a boy
I had a crush on
so many years ago
a boy
who completely
vanished
from memory
until this morning
when he flew
across my mind
whatever happened
to that blue
boy last
I heard
he was headed
for New York
wonder if he landed
in the city
that never sleeps
he dreamed
of being
somebody
a poet

sitting in an ivory tower
looking out a window
on top of the world
I hope he made it
I hope he got lucky
I hope he didn't crash
and burn
I hope he became
a star

Somebody's Son

was stashed in the doorway
like trash nobody had bothered
picking up. A grown man

curled on his side
one arm bent behind his back
at an ungodly angle

as if he were reaching up
to scratch that spot
between the shoulder blades

that's impossible to reach
when you're itchy and alive
one bloodshot eye wide with surprise

somebody's son, whose tongue
was lolling out, whose white skin
was caked with grease and grime

so thick I could have traced
"wash me" on his back
as if he were a sooty moving van

but he was the only unmoving thing
on that hustle bustle street, 5:00 p.m.
corner of Seventh Ave. and West 59th

hordes of people spilling out of buildings
everyone getting off work at once dying
to get home, kick off their heels

loosen their ties, relax with a stiff
one, nobody had a New York minute
to help out somebody's son

who stayed still as a stop sign
as the city swirled around him
his pocked cheek cradling

the sweaty concrete step
his flattened feet folded
like two fallen wings

his faded blue jeans stained and holey
somebody's son, maybe yours?
maybe mine? surely he was somebody's son

once upon a time

Your Loss: To The Lovely Butch In Front Of Me At The A&P

Next time our eyes and hands meet
over the green plastic divider
you slapped down between your organic broccoli
and my politicially incorrect groceries,
before you turn away and dismiss me
so fast, thinking I'm some straight women
bringing these Hungry Man frozen dinners
home for her hubby,
look again honey,
because this chick in her Madonna T-shirt
black mini-skirt
red high heels
with lips and nails to match
may not be wearing a labyris around her neck
or a pink triangle in her ear
but nevertheless would have batted
her incredibly long eyelashes at you
and made some slightly suggestive, sleazy
remark about the gluten-free, sugar-free, dairy-free
yet delicious-looking pair of sticky buns in your basket
if only you'd given her a second glance
and half a chance

Thirteen Ways of Looking at a Poet

I
Among seven silent rooms
Under a moonless midnight sky
The only sound heard
Is the poet's pen
Scritching across the page.

II
The poet was of three minds
Like a sonnet, a sestina
And a terza rima.

III
The poet tried to compose herself
She was a sorry part of the pantomime.

IV
A poet and a poem are one
A poet and a poem and a reader
Are one.

V
The poet does not know
Which to prefer,
Starting a poem
Or ending a poem:
The act of writing
Or the act of having written.

VI
Coffee grows cold in the cup
Lunch lies uneaten on the plate
The poet paces endlessly
Her mood is indecipherable.

VII
Oh young people of the world
With your cell phones, lap tops, and video games
Can't you see the poems waiting to be read
Scattered like fallen leaves all around you?

VIII
The poet knows how to dance the fandango
And bake brownies that can break your heart
But she knows, too
That poetry is involved in everything she knows.

IX
When the poem flew out of the poet's mind
It marked the edge of one of many circles.

X
At the sight of all those poetry collections
On the bookshelves of the library
The poet cried out in ecstasy and despair.

XI
The poet went to a café
And fear overtook her
In that she mistook all the
Latté-sipping patrons for poets.

XII
The poet's pen is moving
The poet must be writing.

XIII
It was the middle of the night
All day long.
The poet was writing
And she was going to write.
The poem sat
In her mind, waiting.

Insomnia

Curled in a heap, I tick off sheep
but I can't sleep at midnight.

My lover's snore, a lion's roar
could start a war at midnight.

A thin moonbeam as white as cream
prevents my dream at midnight.

With any luck and one good fuck
I'll get unstuck at midnight.

I watch the news and get the blues
and cannot snooze at midnight.

Though good for me, a cup of tea
wakes me to pee at midnight.

What is that? Oh, just the cat.
She wants to chat at midnight.

I need a rock to smash the clock
and its tick tock at midnight.

Hands off my breast! Don't be a pest.
I need my rest at midnight.

A car horn blares, my anger flares:
Who dares to honk at midnight?

Wide awake, why did I bake
and eat that cake at midnight?

At least tonight, I tried to write
a poem—goodnight!—it's midnight!

Ode to Chocolate

I need a sweet, I need a treat,
I need to eat some chocolate.

Dark as wood and so damn good,
Oh, I could live on chocolate.

Shaped like a kiss, delivers bliss,
The deep abyss of chocolate.

Just one bite, I'm up all night,
Such is the might of chocolate.

You'll never wed me, never bed me
Till you've fed me chocolate.

I'm sick and sure the only cure
Is more more more pure chocolate.

The smallest bite brings huge delight,
High as a kite from chocolate.

I drink it hot, right from the pot,
What hits the spot? Why, chocolate.

A day without, I'm sure to pout
And then shout, "Where's my chocolate?"

I must confess, I'm one hot mess
Unless I possess chocolate.

Without that cocoa, I go loco,
This ain't no joke—oh chocolate!

Before I dribble, I'll end this scribble,
And go and nibble chocolate!

Ode to a Knish Shop

Mrs. Stahl's sold kasha knishes,
Oy gevalt, were they delicious!
To eat one was to have a feast
for each one weighed a pound at least.
When I was young, they cost a nickel
(cheaper than a kosher pickle).
In Brighton Beach, beneath the el
seduced by that arresting smell,
I'd take the last place in the queue
on Coney Island Avenue,
then perch upon a worn red stool
and try my hardest not to drool,
as I watched Mrs. Stahl herself
pluck knishes from a metal shelf
and serve them piping hot with pride
(the sign outside bragged "Baked Not Fried").
The pastry, bigger than my fist
caressed my tongue, like being kissed.
So savory, so plump, so sweet,
that knish knocked me right off my feet.
The outside dough was parchment-thin
yet strong enough to hold within
buckwheat groats that smelled of earth
and added inches to my girth.
But in those days I didn't care
a whit about my derriére.
That kasha knish was heaven-sent,
no nickel ever better spent.

Ode to Mangoes

I've got to know before I go,
Do mangoes grow in heaven?

Without that treat that tastes so sweet
Don't want no seat in heaven.

If there ain't none—at least a ton—
Won't be no fun in heaven.

Substitute another fruit,
I'll give the boot to heaven.

A mango a day like the good doctor say
And I'll make my way to heaven.

Will a mango slide through my fingers and glide
down my throat as I float up to heaven?

Now say for real, are there mangoes to steal
and peel on the way up to heaven?

If you say no, Lesléa won't go,
No mangoes isn't heaven!

Pear

"You're a pear," said my trainer
as she patted my thighs
which along with my hips
were three times her size.
Somewhat distraught,
I went out and bought
you guessed it—a pear
which I chose with great care.
It was golden and sweet
with a womanly curve,
as I bit it, I thought
she has some nerve!
To call me a pear
and to pat me, to boot,
well I guess it's better
than some damn ugli fruit.

According to Bread

I may be a crusty old heel
full of half-baked ideas
I may loaf around
and do a crummy job

We both know
I always need dough
and more often than not
my life is toast

So tear me apart
eat me alive
swallow me whole
or punch me down

as long as you butter me up
and knead me, honey
whenever you're in a jam
I will rise

PART V: NASTY WOMEN

To Have And To Hold

> *On May 17, 2004, Massachusetts became the first U.S. state to issue marriage licenses to same-sex couples.*

On May 17th, two by two, side by side,
Surrounded by love, we were bursting with pride.
Eager for rights that were so long denied,
On May 17th, two by two, side by side,
Even the newscasters grew misty-eyed
As each groom kissed his groom & each bride kissed her bride.
On May 17th, two by two, side by side,
Surrounded by love, we were bursting with pride.

Seduction In Red

Like six-inch red heels on a Hollywood starlet
Like glistening strawberries baked in a tart
Like elegant nails painted this side of scarlet
Like two strands of rubies worn close to the heart
Like a crystal glass full of expensive red wine
Like a cherry convertible bought on a dare
Like sun-ripe tomatoes too plump for the vine
Like freshly washed shoulder-tossed smooth auburn hair
Like the blush of a bride as she walks down the aisle
Like a bracelet of garnets clasped onto a wrist
Like the lips of a lover curved up in a smile
Like two tender nipples right after they're kissed
Like a crimson silk slip tossed aside in the night
Like that first apple Eve held for Adam to bite

Paradise Found

for Mary

Each night at six the hummingbird
drops by our yard, without a word
you stop with hose in hand and freeze
beneath our acorn-laden trees.
The toy bird takes a dainty drink
(you dare not make a sound or blink)
She flits, she flutters—zip!—she's gone
and you come to and carry on.
You snip, you clip, you tend, you hose
each daisy, lily, heather, rose,
then with your strong and gentle hand
you pluck the fairest of the land.
An ordinary eve as this
could bear not one more drop of bliss.

Night On The Town

When I step into my red silk thong and swivel into the matching
strapless bra my butch bought me for Valentine's Day,

When I slide on my backseam black mesh stockings
sitting on the bed like some Hollywood movie queen,

When I shimmy into my silver sequined mini-dress
that sparkles and turns like a disco ball over a snappy crowd,

When I puff on pink clouds of blush, brush my eyelashes
long and lush, smear my lips richer than ruby red,

When I step into sky high heels, snap on shiny earrings
and slip seventeen silver bracelets halfway up my arm,

When I dab my shoulders and neck, earlobes and wrists
clevage and thighs with thick, musky perfume,

When I curl my hair into ringlets that dip over one eye
and bounce off my shoulder like some Clairol girl gone wild,

When I turn from the mirror, pick up my purse
and finally announce that I'm ready to go,

When my butch kickbangs the door, takes me
in her arms and whispers, "Why don't we just stay home tonight,"

When I sigh and pout, "But we never go out," while she shushes
me with kisses and leads me right back to the bedroom

Where she has her way with me and I have my way with her
as if that wasn't my plan all along.

I Want To Stay Up Talking But

You kiss me at midnight and tell me to hush
I lie back in bed and do just as you say
Feeling my cheeks and my chest start to blush
You kiss me at midnight and tell me to hush
Then make it quite clear that you're not in a rush
The new year is here and we're happy and gay
You kiss me at midnight and tell me to hush
I lie back in bed and do just as you say

The Coming Storm

Outside sheets of rain
Inside sheets of satin

Outside pounding sleet
Inside pounding hearts

Outside temperatures fall
Inside temperatures rise

Outside bare branches
Inside naked limbs

Outside shivering with cold
Inside quivering with heat

Outside slick roads
Inside slick skin

Outside heavy snow
Inside heavy breathing

Outside slippery sidewalks
Inside slippery fingers

Outside glistening fields
Inside glistening bodies

Outside howl of wind
Inside howl of joy

Outside nasty weather
Inside nasty women

Love Shampoo

gleams in your palm
a dollop of opal moon
slathered, it lathers
you into a Roman goddess
a marvel of marble
sleek, slender, and smooth
all your worries whirling
and swirling down the drain

refreshed and dressed
you seize the day   don't
be surprised if you turn
heads as you saunter down the street
there has never been anyone
more lovely than you

Ghazal For My Beloved

Each night in our bed as I face my beloved.
I open my arms and embrace my beloved.

Her skin smooth as sand on a tropical isle,
My hands swoop and swirl as I trace my beloved.

Remember that night long ago in the park,
When the moon watched us go to first base, my beloved?

I'll run like the young girl I was long ago,
If you promise that you will give chase, my beloved.

Is there a more glorious sight to behold,
than us in our leather and lace, my beloved?

In a dyke bar ten butches, each handsome and fine.
Which one of them makes my heart race? My beloved.

Women spin round me as countless as stars,
But no one on earth can displace my beloved.

Two decades ago, when you whispered, "Be mine,"
I gave you my heart, Mary Grace, my beloved.

What I Love   *for Mary Grace Newman Vazquez*

the thick black curls rising and falling
all over your head like the waves
of the Caribbean Sea surrounding
the island the day you were born;

your dark Spanish eyes that widen
with surprise each time I climb
aboard the boat of your body
and happily drift away;

the wide plain of your Taino cheeks
your nose and chin, your lopsided
grin that warms me all over
like a tropical sun;

your small brown hands that recognize
what hides inside a piece of wood:
a dolphin, a porpoise, a whale waiting
to leap out at the kiss of your knife;

your long strong arms
that pin me to your chest
my hammock, my haven,
my place of rest;

your solid tree trunk torso
your strong upright piano legs
your small sweet Puerto Rican feet
that plant you firmly beside me;

and how could I forget
the African drum of your heart
that called me called me called me
and carried me carried me home.

The Writer And The Messenger

a birthday poem for Mary

The Writer and the Messenger
were walking hand in hand,
their faces turned up toward the sun
their feet down in the sand,
their eyes as bright as stars at night
their cheeks so nicely tanned.

"The time has come," the Writer said,
"to talk of Mary V."
The Messenger stood tall and proud
and said aloud, "That's me!"
"Our story," said the Writer,
"starts in nineteen-forty-three."

That third September Saturday
was sunny and quite warm.
No clouds were high up in the sky,
no sign of rain or storm.
A perfect Puerto Rican day
for Alicia to be born.

Placed up in a hammock
that was tied between two trees,
she swayed back and forth and back again
rocked by an island breeze.
"Por favor, some Dramamine,"
Alicia whispered. "Please."

A few years passed and then at last
it was adoption day.
Alicia, now called Mary
and her mama sailed away.
"Now may I have some Dramamine?"
The answer still was nay.

She grew up in Northampton
and when high school days were done,
She said, "I know just where to go,
I know what would be fun.
I think I'll move to Lexington
and be a little nun."

And though it was forbidden,
a particular friend she had.
Her name was Sister Mary Lee
and sister, she was bad.
They sent her to Toledo
which made Sister Vazquez sad.

She returned to our fair city
and went back to her old tricks,
now working as a nurse's aide
upstairs at Cooley Dick's
and along with Faye the D.J.
spinning records for La Mix.

Then one day our Mary
heard a loud and desperate call:
"We need a city messenger,
someone to shlep and haul."
Said Mary V., "That job's for me.
I know I'll have a ball."

The years flew by, then Mary
said to Perfect Cat one night,
"I think I'll take myself a class.
I'd like to learn to write."
And when she met the teacher
it was true love at first sight.

The Writer and the Messenger
stood by a sea of blue.
The Messenger said, "Look my love.
Do you admire the view?"
The Writer said, "Not half as much
as I admire you."

"Playing softball, spinning records,
planting bulbs of every hue,
taking photos, clowning, improv,
carving wood and Feng Shui too.
With breakneck speed how you succeed
in everything you do."

"You've taught me to appreciate
the turtle and the dove.
You've taught me to look up at night
and watch the stars above.
But most of all," the Writer said,
"you've taught me how to love."

So happy birthday, baby.
May your wishes all come true.
May your days be filled with laughter,
May your tears and fears be few.
May your years be good and plenty,
May I spend them all with you.

Why I Always Wear Makeup

Because on the day I leave earth
and this face I call mine,
I want to remember them both
as divine

Notes

Page 1: "Thirteen Ways Of Looking At A Blackboard" was inspired by "Thirteen Ways of Looking at a Blackbird" by Wallace Stevens from *The Collected Works of Wallace Stevens* (New York: Knopf, 1954).

Page 12: "Maidel" was inspired by "Girl" by Jamaica Kincaid from *At The Bottom Of The River* (New York: Aventura, The Vintage Library of Contemporary World Literature, 1985).

Page 33: "Old Age" was inspired by "The Span of Life" by Robert Frost from *A Further Range* (New York: Henry Holt, 1936).

Page 64: "Thirteen Ways Of Looking At A Poet" was inspired by "Thirteen Ways of Looking at a Blackbird" by Wallace Stevens from *The Collected Works of Wallace Stevens* (New York: Knopf, 1954).

Page 86: "The Writer And The Messenger" was inspired by "The Walrus and The Carpenter" by Lewis Carroll from *Through the Looking Glass and What Alice Found There* (London: MacMillan & Company, 1872).

Acknowledgements

Print Journals and Magazines
Moment Magazine: "The Chanukah Game"
Naugatuck River Review: "First Death"
Silkworm: "May Day"
Spoon River Poetry Review: "Viet Nam"

Anthologies
Nasty Women Poets: An Unapologetic Anthology of Subversive Verse (Lost Horse Press, 2017): "The Coming Storm"
Soap Opera Confidential: Writers and Soap Insiders on Why We'll Tune in Tomorrow as the World Turns Restlessly by the Guiding Light of Our Lives. (McFarland & Company, 2017): "My Mother's Stories"

Online Journals
Festival Writer: "Sleepaway Camp, 1969"
IthacaLit: "Between Flights"
Lavender Review: "Paradise Found," "I Want To Stay Up Talking But"
Napalm Health Spa: "First Death"
Persimmon Tree: "Maidel"
Mezzo Cammin: "Thirteen Ways of Looking At A Poet," "Why I Always Wear Makeup," "My Mother Cups Her Hand"
Solstice Literary Magazine: "Poem for Two Dogs Hanged in Salem, Massachusetts, 1692" (second place runner-up in contest judged by Terrance Hayes)

The author wishes to thank Mary Meriam and Risa Denenberg of Headmistress Press; Elizabeth Harding and Sarah Gerton of Curtis Brown, Ltd.; and first readers Ann Turner, Barbara Diamond Goldin, Corinne Demas, Ellen Wittlinger, Ellen LaFleche, Jane Yolen, and Patricia MacLachlan. And lastly but not leastly, undying gratitude to Mary Grace Newman Vazquez for the lovely life we share.

Photo by Mary Vazquez

About The Author

Lesléa Newman has created 70 books for readers of all ages including the poetry collections *I Carry My Mother* which was named a 2016 "Must Read" title by the Massachusetts Center for the Book and received the 2016 Golden Crown Literary Society Poetry Award, and *October Mourning: A Song for Matthew Shepard* which received the 2013 American Library Association Stonewall Honor and the 2014 Florida Council of Teachers of English Joan F. Kaywell Books Save Lives Award. Other titles include the children's books *Heather Has Two Mommies* and *Sparkle Boy*; the short story collections, *Girls Will Be Girls*, and *A Letter to Harvey Milk*; and the writing guide, *Write from the Heart*. Her literary awards include poetry fellowships from the National Endowment for the Arts and the Massachusetts Artists Foundation. Nine of her books have been Lambda Literary Award finalists. From 2008 -2010, she served as the poet laureate of Northampton, MA. Currently she is a faculty member of Spalding University's low-residency MFA in Writing program.

Headmistress Press Books

Teeth & Teeth - Robin Reagler
How Distant the City - Freesia McKee
Shopgirls - Marissa Higgins
Riddle - Diane Fortney
When She Woke She Was an Open Field - Hilary Brown
God With Us - Amy Lauren
A Crown of Violets - Renée Vivien tr. Samantha Pious
Fireworks in the Graveyard - Joy Ladin
Social Dance - Carolyn Boll
The Force of Gratitude - Janice Gould
Spine - Sarah Caulfield
Diatribe from the Library - Farrell Greenwald Brenner
Blind Girl Grunt - Constance Merritt
Acid and Tender - Jen Rouse
Beautiful Machinery - Wendy DeGroat
Odd Mercy - Gail Thomas
The Great Scissor Hunt - Jessica K. Hylton
A Bracelet of Honeybees - Lynn Strongin
Whirlwind @ Lesbos - Risa Denenberg
The Body's Alphabet - Ann Tweedy
First name Barbie last name Doll - Maureen Bocka
Heaven to Me - Abe Louise Young
Sticky - Carter Steinmann
Tiger Laughs When You Push - Ruth Lehrer
Night Ringing - Laura Foley
Paper Cranes - Dinah Dietrich
On Loving a Saudi Girl - Carina Yun
The Burn Poems - Lynn Strongin
I Carry My Mother - Lesléa Newman
Distant Music - Joan Annsfire
The Awful Suicidal Swans - Flower Conroy
Joy Street - Laura Foley
Chiaroscuro Kisses - G.L. Morrison
The Lillian Trilogy - Mary Meriam
Lady of the Moon - Amy Lowell, Lillian Faderman, Mary Meriam
Irresistible Sonnets - ed. Mary Meriam
Lavender Review - ed. Mary Meriam

www.ingramcontent.com/pod-product-compliance
Lightning Source LLC
Chambersburg PA
CBHW071146090426
42736CB00012B/2254